Overview *Fly Like the Eagle*

One day the librarian who is helping Riley learn to read is not there.

Reading Vocabulary Words

gold   pale
librarian

High-Frequency Words

hello   today
bed   visit
fly   up
sat   library

Building Future Vocabulary

* These vocabulary words do not appear in this text. They are provided to develop related oral vocabulary that first appears in future texts.

Words:	*hero*	*concern*	*heal*
Levels:	Gold	Gold	Gold

Comprehension Strategy
Rereading text

Fluency Skill
Reading exclamatory sentences in an excited manner

Phonics Skill
Using knowledge of spelling patterns to decode: CVC (big, his, had, was, bus)

Reading-Writing Connection
Copying a phrase

Send home one of the Flying Colors Take-Home books for children to share with their families.

Differentiated Instruction
Before reading the text, query children to discover their level of understanding of the comprehension strategy — Rereading text. As you work together, provide additional support to children who show a beginning mastery of the strategy.

Focus on ELL
- Introduce the concept of a library. Discuss what you can find in a library, and show examples of these items. Help children use the correct English terms.

- Talk about librarians and what they do in their jobs.

Using This Teaching Version

1. Before Reading

2. During Reading

3. Revisiting the Text

4. Assessment

This Teaching Version will assist you in directing children through the process of reading.

1. **Begin with Before Reading** to familiarize children with the book's content. Select the skills and strategies that meet the needs of your children.

2. **Next, go to During Reading** to help children become familiar with the text, and then to read individually on their own.

3. **Then, go back to Revisiting the Text** and select those specific activities that meet children's needs.

4. Finally, finish with Assessment to confirm children are ready to move forward to the next text.

Building Background

• Write the word *gold* on the board. Read it aloud. Ask children to point to something in the room that is gold. Ask *What does it mean to be "as good as gold"?* (to be healthy, or to be in good shape)

• Introduce the book by reading the title, talking about the cover illustration, and sharing the overview.

Building Future Vocabulary
Use Interactive Modeling Card: Meaning Map

• On the Meaning Map, write the word *hero* and the sentence *The firefighter was a hero*.

• Work with children to complete the Meaning Map. You may want to ask a volunteer to find the word *hero* in a dictionary.

Introduction to Reading Vocabulary

• On blank cards write: *gold*, *librarian*, and *pale*. Read them aloud. Tell children these words will appear in the text of *Fly Like the Eagle*.

• Use each word in a sentence for understanding.

Introduction to Comprehension Strategy

- Explain that sometimes, part of a story may not be clear when we read it. We may need to go back and reread to understand it better.

- Tell children they will be rereading the text to help them understand *Fly Like the Eagle.*

- Using the cover illustration, ask children if they can predict where the story takes place.

Introduction to Phonics

- Write CVC on the board and explain the Consonant-Vowel-Consonant pattern. Write the words **leg**, **his**, and **had** on the board and point out the CVC pattern.

- Explain that this story has many three-letter words that follow this CVC pattern. Have children turn to page 2 and locate the word **big**. Ask *Does this word fit the CVC pattern?*

- Have children look for other words with the CVC pattern as they read *Fly Like the Eagle.*

Modeling Fluency

- Have children follow along as you read aloud the last paragraph on page 4, modeling excitement.

- Point out the exclamation point and explain that it shows excitement.

2 During Reading

Book Talk
Beginning on page T4, use the During Reading notes on the left-hand side to engage children in a book talk. On page 16, follow with Individual Reading.

Book Talk

- **Comprehension Strategy**
  Have children look at the cover illustration. Ask *Who is on the cover?* (a boy and a woman) *Is the woman reading to the boy, or is it the other way around?* (The woman is reading to the boy.)

- Have children read the chapter titles on the title page. Say *Someone disappears in the story. Who do you think disappears?* (Mrs. Canon) *Why do you think that?* (because one of the chapters is called "Where Is Mrs. Canon?")

Turn to page 2 – Book Talk

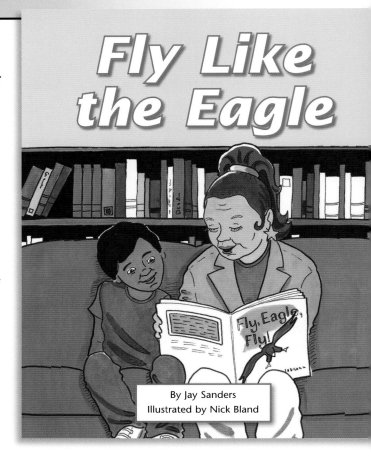

Fly Like the Eagle

By Jay Sanders
Illustrated by Nick Bland

Fly Like the Eagle

By Jay Sanders
Illustrated by Nick Bland

Future Vocabulary

• Have children look at the cover illustration. Ask *What is Mrs. Canon doing?* (reading to Riley) *What does she want Riley to do?* (learn to read) *Is Mrs. Canon concerned about whether Riley learns to read?*

Now revisit pages 2–3

During Reading

Book Talk

- Ask *Where does this story take place?* (in a library) *Who is the woman behind the counter?* (the librarian) *Who might be the older man with Riley?* (Grandpa)

- Have children read page 2. Ask *What does Mrs. Canon mean when she says she is "as good as gold"?* (She is well; she is fine.)

- **Phonics Skill** Have children find the word *big* on page 2 and identify the consonant, vowel, and consonant.

Turn to page 4 — Book Talk

Chapter 1

Good as Gold

"Hello, Mrs. Canon," said Riley as he pushed open the big glass doors. "How are you today?"

"As good as gold, Riley," smiled Mrs. Canon, the librarian, "as good as gold."

2

Future Vocabulary

- Say *The people are sitting on the lawn. Do you have a lawn where you live? Most parks and schools have a lawn area. How are lawns taken care of? What needs to be done to maintain a lawn?* (It needs to be mowed, watered, and fertilized.)

Now revisit pages 4–5

During Reading

Book Talk

- **Comprehension Strategy**
  Have children read the first paragraph on page 4. Ask *What do we learn about Lara on this page?* (She is blind.) *What opinions have you formed about Lara now that you know she is blind? Why?*

- Point out the word *blind* on these pages. Say *This word tells us that Lara cannot see. That is why she put her hand on her mom's arm as they went down the steps.*

- Say *People are carrying blankets and picnic baskets to the outdoor concert. Concerts in the park are often held in nice weather. People sit on blankets and enjoy the music.* Have children share outdoor concert experiences.

Turn to page 6 – Book Talk

Lara put her hand on Mom's arm as they went down the steps because Lara was blind.

On the way to the park, they met lots of other children and parents. They were going to the concert, too.

Some of the parents carried chairs and blankets to sit on.

"This is going to be the best concert we have ever had," said Pete. "This year we are having it in the park for the first time."

4

Future Vocabulary

• Have children locate and point to the girl in pink on this page. Say *She is wearing a skirt. What is a skirt?* (a piece of clothing that is worn from the waist down) Identify any children wearing skirts in the class. Say *Look at Pete and Lara's mom. She is wearing a dress. How is a skirt different from a dress?* (A dress goes down from the shoulders; a skirt starts at the waist.)

Now revisit pages 6–7

During Reading

Book Talk

- Have children look at the illustrations. Say *Look at the groups of people waiting for the concert to begin. Some families are visiting. Two children are playing a hand game while they wait.* Discuss activities children do while they wait.

- Guide children to point to the two adults near the stage. Say *It looks as though they are whispering. What do you think they are discussing?* (when to start the concert, whether everyone has arrived)

Turn to page 8 — Book Talk

Chapter 2

Waiting for the Concert to Begin

When they got to the park,
Pete ran to sit with the other children.

Mom put the blanket on the grass,
and Lara sat down with her.

Everyone waited.

Soon it was time for the concert to begin.

Everyone waited . . . and waited.

6

Future Vocabulary

- Say *Many people play lawn games. Have you ever played bocce or croquet? These are fun lawn games played with balls. In croquet, you use a mallet to hit balls through small hoops. In bocce, you try to throw your heavy ball closest to a small marker ball.*

Now revisit pages 8–9

During Reading

Book Talk

- Read page 8 aloud. Ask *Who is at the microphone?* (Mr. Jacobs) *What is he saying?* (Mrs. Forest's car broke down; she is the piano player; the concert can't start yet.) *How are the people in the audience handling this announcement?* (The people look surprised and interested; a baby cries.)

- **Phonics Skill** Have children identify two contractions on page 8. *(I'm, can't)* Remind them of the list of contractions you made earlier in the lesson.

- Have children locate the word *concert* on these pages.

Turn to page 10 — Book Talk

Then Mr. Jacobs, one of the teachers, said, "I'm sorry, everyone.
We can't start the concert yet
because Mrs. Forest is going to be late.
Her car has broken down.
Mrs. Forest plays the piano for us."

Everyone waited . . . and waited
. . . and waited.

8

9

Future Vocabulary

- Have children locate the baby in the illustration. Say *The baby is upset on this page. When someone is upset, they are unhappy. Why might the baby be upset?* (tired, hungry, wet)

Now revisit pages 10–11

During Reading

Book Talk

- Say *Mrs. Forest's car won't start.* Discuss what Mrs. Forest will do and ways she could still get to the concert.

- Say *The illustration on these pages shows Mr. Jacobs and the children who are performing in the concert. How do you think the children feel?* (sad, nervous, eager for Mrs. Forest to get there) *Why do you think they feel this way?* (They want to put on the concert; they have been practicing.)

- **Phonics Skill** Have children point to and identify two contractions on page 10. *(won't, don't)*

Turn to page 12 — Book Talk

After a long time, Mr. Jacobs said, "Mrs. Forest has just phoned me to say that her car won't start at all."

"Oh, no!" cried the children. "We want to have the concert. We don't want to go home yet!"

"Can anyone help us, please?" asked Mr. Jacobs.

10

Future Vocabulary

- Say *The people at this concert are* upset *because the concert is delayed.* The word upset has other meanings, too. You might hear a sports announcer say: *The team that was not expected to win came from behind to win the game; it was an* upset. *In this case,* upset means "beat unexpectedly."

- Say *Mrs. Forest can't make it to the concert. Maybe Mrs. Forest lives on the out*skirts *of town. Have you ever heard the word* outskirts? Outskirts *means "the outer edge or the outer part of town."*

Now revisit pages 12–13

During Reading

Book Talk

- Say *Some musicians can play by ear. That means they can simply hear something and then play it. Do you think this would be hard to do? Why or why not?*

Turn to page 14 – Book Talk

Chapter 3

Lara Helps Out

Pete jumped up and said,
"Mr. Jacobs, my sister Lara can play the piano.
She could play it for us."

"Your sister can't play the piano!"
whispered one of the big boys.
"She's blind."

"My sister doesn't need to see the music,"
said Pete.
"She is so clever she can play the piano
without it."

12

13

Future Vocabulary

- Say *We know people can be upset, but objects can also be upset. Imagine you are carrying a basket of apples. Now imagine a dog runs by and upsets your basket and the apples tumble out. Here, upset means "overturn" or "force out."*

Now revisit pages 14–15

During Reading

Book Talk

- Say *Lara agrees to play the piano for the concert. How do you think she knows the songs?* (She has heard Pete practice.) Point to the last sentence on page 14. Ask *Why do you think the children shouted, More, more?* (They were having fun; they wanted to keep dancing and singing.)

- Have children locate and point to the word *concert*.

Turn to page 16 — Book Talk

Lara smiled and said,
"I would like to play the piano
for your concert, Pete."

Mom helped Lara over to the piano.

Lara knew all the songs.
Pete had been singing them at home.

Lara began to play the piano,
and the children started to sing.

They sang all of the songs,
and they danced all of the dances.

"More! More!" shouted the children.

14

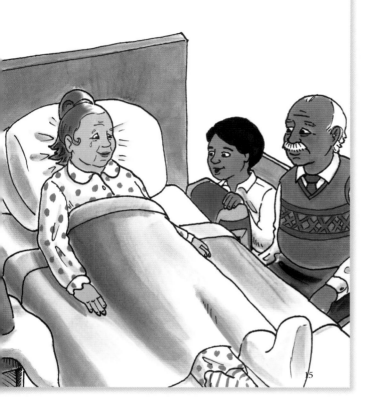

Future Vocabulary
- Tell children that they can learn about the characters in a book by paying attention to their actions. Ask *What things have Riley's grandparents done?* (Grandpa takes Riley to the library every Friday, and he brings Riley to the hospital. Grandma expresses concern about Mrs. Canon, bakes her a cake, and comes to the hospital.) *What do these actions tell you about Riley's grandparents?* (They are kind; they are concerned about other people.)

- Remind children that people can be heroes by doing the right thing. Ask *How can Mrs. Canon be a hero to Riley?* (by taking good care of herself so her leg heals)

Go to page T5 —
Revisiting the Text

During Reading

Book Talk

- Leave this page for children to discover on their own when they read the book individually.

Individual Reading

Have each child read the entire book at his or her own pace while remaining in the group.

**Go to page T5 —
Revisiting the Text**

Riley took *Fly, Eagle, Fly!* out of his backpack and began to read.

He read each word very carefully, just as he had practiced the night before with Grandpa.

When the last sentence was finished, he looked up at Mrs. Canon and smiled.

"Riley," she said returning his smile, "I'm very proud of you. I always knew one day you would fly like the eagle!"

During independent work time, children can read the online book at:
www.rigbyflyingcolors.com

Revisiting the Text

Future Vocabulary

- Use the notes on the right-hand pages to develop oral vocabulary that goes beyond the text. These vocabulary words first appear in future texts. These words are: *hero*, *concern*, and *heal*.

  Turn back to page 1

Reading Vocabulary Review

Activity Sheet: Sentence Maker

- Write the word *gold* on the board. Have a volunteer read it aloud.

- Have children fill in the top of the Sentence Maker with the word *gold*. Ask children to think of phrases and a sentence to complete the chart.

Comprehension Strategy Review

Use Interactive Modeling Card: Comparing Two Fiction Books

- Brainstorm with children another fiction book the class has read that reminds them of *Fly Like the Eagle*.

- Complete the chart by filling in the columns for each book.

Phonics Review

- Discuss vowels and consonants. With children, search the text for three-letter CVC words and list them on the board.

- Review this list, then ask children to write a sentence for each word on the list.

Fluency Review

- Partner children and have them take turns reading the sentences on pages 10 and 11 in the text.

- Remind children to read sentences ending with an exclamation point with excitement as a way to build drama.

Reading-Writing Connection

Activity Sheet: Story Map

To assist children with linking reading and writing:

- Review the parts of the Story Map and have children complete it for *Fly Like the Eagle*.

- Wherever possible, have children copy phrases from the text to complete their Story Map.

4 Assessment

Assessing Future Vocabulary

Work with each child individually. Ask questions that elicit each child's understanding of the Future Vocabulary words. Note each child's responses:

- How does someone become a hero?
- Which concerns your life more: the cleanliness of your classroom, or how much bananas cost in Canada?
- Which will take longer to heal: a scratch or a broken leg?

Assessing Comprehension Strategy

Work with each child individually. Note each child's understanding of rereading text:

- What happened to Mrs. Canon?
- What did Riley want to do when he learned Mrs. Canon was in the hospital?
- What was the special surprise Riley had for Mrs. Canon?
- What should you do if you don't understand what's going on in a story?

Assessing Phonics

Work with each child individually. Turn to page 3 and have each child read this page aloud. Note each child's responses for understanding how to decode the spelling pattern CVC:

- Did each child recognize consonants and vowels?
- Did each child recognize when words fit the CVC pattern?
- Point to the word *the* and ask each child if this word fits the CVC pattern.

Assessing Fluency

Have each child read page 16 to you. Note each child's understanding of using exclamation points to show excitement:

- Did each child model excitement when reading the sentences or phrases that ended in exclamation points?
- Did each child read the remaining sentences in a normal tone of voice?

Interactive Modeling Cards

Meaning Map

hero	The firefighter was a hero.
Word	Sentence

I think the word means: someone who does something brave

The definition I found: a brave person

A new sentence that shows the meaning: My mom is a hero because she fixes dinner even when she's tired.

Directions: With children, fill in the Meaning Map using the word *hero*.

Comparing Two Fiction Books

	Book Title *Fly Like the Eagle*	Book Title *Going Home*
Setting in Time and Place	library, modern	country, past
Main Character	Riley, kind and thoughtful	Dorothy, brave, kind
Story Problem	Riley is concerned about Mrs. Canon's leg.	Dorothy wants to go home.
How the Character Handles the Problem	visits Mrs. Canon in the hospital	faces challenges but keeps going
Solution	he shows her he cares	gets people to help her

Directions: With children, fill in the Comparing Two Fiction Books chart.

Discussion Questions

- What book did Mrs. Canon read to Riley? (Literal)
- Why did Riley visit Mrs. Canon in the hospital? (Critical Thinking)
- Why do you think Riley learned to read by the time he visited Mrs. Canon in the hospital? (Inferential)

Activity Sheets

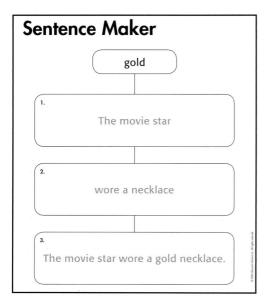

Sentence Maker

gold

1. The movie star

2. wore a necklace

3. The movie star wore a gold necklace.

Directions: Have children fill in the Sentence Maker using the word *gold*.

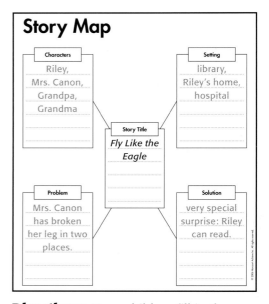

Story Map

Characters
Riley,
Mrs. Canon,
Grandpa,
Grandma

Setting
library,
Riley's home,
hospital

Story Title
Fly Like the Eagle

Problem
Mrs. Canon has broken her leg in two places.

Solution
very special surprise: Riley can read.

Directions: Have children fill in the Story Map, copying phrases from *Fly Like the Eagle* wherever appropriate.
Optional: Have children write a story in which they use the phrase "as good as gold."